Sounds of the Heart, Volume 1 : Prayers for Musicians
Copyright © 2020 by Trent Phillips

All rights reserved. Printed in the United States of America. No part of this book may be used or reproduced in any manner whatsoever without written permission except in the case of brief quotations embodied in critical articles or reviews.

Ordering Information:
Quantity sales: Special discounts are available on quantity purchases by corporations, associations, and others.
For details, email: info@trentphillips.com.

Published by :
Relentless Publishing House, LLC
www.relentlesspublishing.com

Cover and graphic design by Justin Foster
www.jus10foster.com

ISBN: 978-1-948829-78-6

10 9 8 7 6 5 4 3 2 1

DEDICATION

To my wife, Brittany - for sharing both the joys and weight of this vision and stepping in to help me to see things with new eyes - thank you! I value your listening ear and your brilliant contributions to this work. You always make sure I'm on point! I love you!

To my family, Mom & Dad - Leon, Sr. and Helen Phillips - thank you for the consistent encouragement to do and be anything. I'm continually striving to make you both proud! Michael, you inspire me in ways you won't believe.
I'm honored to call you my brother. Mom Janice, Dad Tim, Anya, Ben, and Zhaleh thanks for your support.
Love you all!

To all of my musician friends, colleagues, and supporters around the world who inspire me and challenge me every day to be a greater version of myself... Thank you!
This is for *you*.

TABLE OF CONTENTS

Foreword	8
Introduction	11
Seeker's Prayer	14
Gratitude Prayer	16
Wisdom & Guidance	18
Faith	20
Petition (Needs & Wants)	22
Use Me For Your Glory	24
Maturity (For The Young Adult)	26
Professionalism	28
Integrity	30
Creativity	32
My Affirmation: Creativity	35
Proper Alignment (Priorities)	36
Relationship With God	38
Relationship With Others	40
Focus (Mindfulness)	42
Discipline	44
My Affirmation: Discipline	47
Fear	48
Pride	50
Forgiveness	52
Expansion (Something Greater)	54

Finances	56
My Affirmation: Finances	59
Singleness	60
Marriage (For Spouses)	62
As A Parent	64
As A Leader	66
For A Friend	68
For My Family	70
True Success	72
Influence	74
My Affirmation: Influence	77
Healing (For Sickness & Disease)	78
Depression	80
Suicidal Thoughts	82
Overcoming Addictions	84
Confidence In My Identity (Low Self Image)	86
My Affirmation: Confidence	89
A Musician's Prayer	91
Acknowledgements	93
About the Author	95

FOREWORD

Ephesians 4:8 famously states, "That is why the Scriptures say, 'When He ascended to the heights, He led a crowd of captives and gave gifts to His people.'" The Scripture that Paul is quoting is Psalms 68:18, which says that the reason he gave gifts to his people is "...so that the Lord may dwell among them."

Your gift was given to you so that wherever you use it, the Lord would have permission to manifest himself and work there. This reason alone causes a crisis in the life of every gifted person in the Body of Christ. There is often an unexplained heaviness that usually accompanies giftedness. And that is because the devil would love nothing more than to hinder or harm the vessel that houses the gift.

In this book, Trent Phillips has set out to inspire and equip those commonly referred to as "Creatives" with the tools necessary to withstand the pressures of a life of giftedness. He has chosen to instruct Creatives on how to use the weapon of Prayer to create a connection with God and have balance in life so that the gift you carry won't crush you.

Use this book as a tool to facilitate and strengthen your prayer life. It will pay great dividends in the days, weeks, months and years to come as these prayers sink down into your heart, become your way of expressing yourself to God, and ascend with authority to the One who made you specifically for His purpose.

-Dr. Hart Ramsey
Pastor, Northview Christian Church

INTRODUCTION

Have you ever been stuck in a mental space where you didn't know how to pray? Or maybe you knew what you needed to pray about but just couldn't find the words! I've been there many times. Sometimes life causes us to shut down and clam up to the point that we can't articulate what we feel, need, or want.

One of the greatest moments in my life was when I discovered that God truly hears our hearts and knows our thoughts before we think or speak of them! Everything began to change when I learned that prayer was "my space" with God, and that I could always be myself, release the pressure, and say what I need to say.

I was inspired to create this resource to aid in your journey towards a lifestyle of prayer, where we as "creatives" to connect our hearts to the heart of God, letting the sound of our hearts be heard by Him.

It is my hope that this book will be a tremendous blessing and that you will share it with someone else.

-*Trent Phillips*

WHAT COMES FROM THE HEART GOES TO THE HEART.

-SAMUEL TAYLOR COLERIDGE

Sounds of the Heart, Volume 1: Prayers for Musicians

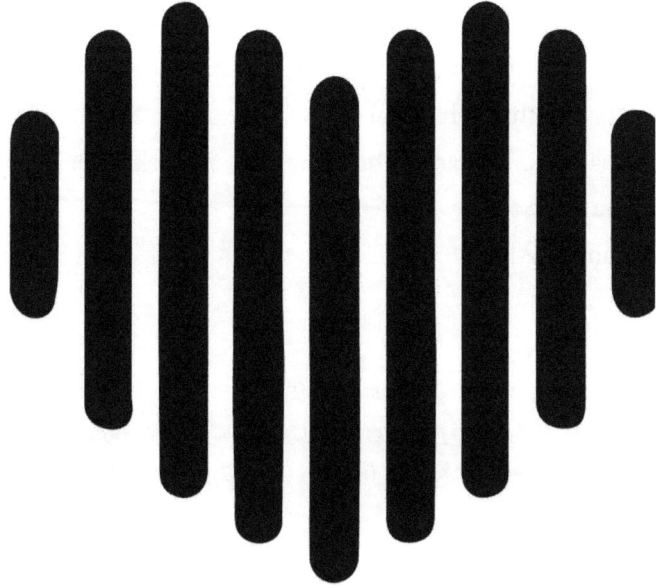

Seeker's Prayer

GOD, if You're real, I'm reaching out to You. I'm not sure of any of this, but I'm taking a step in Your direction. Please show me that You're real and not just a figment of my imagination. Reveal Yourself to me through Your Word, the Holy Spirit, this book, people, situations, and any other way that You choose. I am open to what You have to say.
In Jesus' name... Amen.

Acts 17:27 TPT
"He has done this so that every person would long for God, feel their way to him, and find him—for he is the God who is easy to discover!"

REFLECTIONS

Growing up in a Christian home and going to church regularly with my family allowed me the opportunity to see God from a certain perspective. I also was dunked head first into organized religion – which I've learned over the years isn't a bad thing, when rooted in the right foundation and principles. I wasn't skeptical of the existence of "God", but being a 'Why?' child, I often wondered about the reasoning behind lots of the religious customs I would witness and most times be asked or trained to participate in. One day, when my curiosity peaked, I took a step in God's direction, and He showed me (and continues to show me) who He really is!

- Reflect on your personal story of searching for God. Feel free to write your thoughts below.

_____

_____

_____

Gratitude Prayer

GOD, thank You for life. Thank You for allowing me to see this brand new day. Thank You for all of the awesome moments as well as those that You've allowed to develop me. Thank You for Your faithfulness and love towards me. I am so grateful for how You supply my needs and grant my desires. I'm thankful for my family and close friends. Thank You for the blessing of health and strength. Thank You for resources, safety, and protection. Thank you, Lord, for the gift of music and the gift of creativity. I will continue to express my gratitude for every experience. Amen!

1 Thessalonians 5:17-18 NRSV
"Pray without ceasing, give thanks in all circumstances; for this is the will of God in Christ Jesus for you."

REFLECTIONS

Gratitude is something that requires intentionality. Being grateful is a state of mind, both sparked and maintained by a series of decisions. I didn't learn the true power of gratitude until a couple of years ago, in my late 30's. (Wow! How much time was wasted being negative?!) Gratefulness sets off a universal law that commands great things to come to us... it's like a magnet! Waking up every day saying, "Thank You for life and being able to see this amazing day" is just the beginning.

What else are you grateful for? How can you maintain your state of gratitude throughout the entire day?

_____

_____

_____

Wisdom & Guidance

GOD, thank You for wisdom that only comes from You. When I am confused, stressed, and overwhelmed with questions, I can run to You to find strength and clarity. Your word says "In all your ways acknowledge Him and He will direct your paths", so help me to consult You in every decision. Please show me what doors to enter and which doors to stay away from. Holy Spirit, lead and guide me. Help me to slow down enough to listen and apply the information that You've already given me. Thank You for Your divine direction! In Jesus' name... Amen.

Proverbs 3:6 NLT
"Seek His will in all you do and He will show you which path to take."

Proverbs 2:2-4 NLT
"Tune your ears to wisdom, and concentrate on understanding. Cry out for insight, and ask for understanding. Search for them as you would for silver; seek them like hidden treasures."

REFLECTIONS

How many times have we moved without praying about it first? I believe most of us have. It's in our human nature to want to be independent and feel self-sufficient, even apart from our Creator. I have learned through making mistakes to include God in every decision so that His wisdom can rule my mind. It's a challenge, but it's one that's worth the effort!

Accept this challenge with me... Consult God in prayer. You'll find the answer!

_____

_____

_____

Faith

GOD, I ask You for increased faith. Help me to believe in who You've made me to be and trust what You've said about me. Help me see through the eyes of hope, the dreams You've placed in my heart, and that they can actually come true. I admit that sometimes these things are difficult for me to grasp, so I ask that You would increase my capacity to believe. Help me to please Your heart by exhibiting great faith in You. In Jesus' name... Amen.

Hebrews 11:1 NKJV
"Now faith is the substance of things hoped for, the evidence of things not seen."

Hebrews 11:6 NKJV
"But without faith it is impossible to please Him, for he who comes to God must believe that He is, and that He is a rewarder for those who diligently seek Him."

REFLECTIONS

Faith is defined as confidence or trust in a person or thing. It is also defined as "belief". The Bible explains that faith is given to <u>everyone</u> upon existence, and that it's something that needs to be fed and grow over time and through experience. We exhibit faith every day in various ways and often don't realize it. When it comes to trusting God, why does it seem so hard to use this valuable tool when in fact we already have it?

List some areas of your life that you struggle in your faith. Then, be intent to give these areas over to God daily in prayer.

_____

_____

_____

Petition (Needs & Wants)

GOD, I pray this prayer of petition for [insert what you need here]. Your Word instructs us to Ask, Seek, and Knock and I am doing just that. You've promised that if we abide in You and Your words abide in us, we can ask anything according to Your Will and it will be given. I pray this in faith, believing that I've already received what is in Your perfect will for my life. Thank You, Lord, for being so mindful of me and everything that concerns me. I praise You in advance. In Jesus' name... Amen.

Luke 11:9-10 NRSV
"So I say to you, Ask, and it will be given you; search, and you will find; knock, and the door will be opened for you. For everyone who asks receives, and everyone who searches finds, and for everyone who knocks, the door
will be opened."

John 15:7 NRSV
"If you abide in me, and my words abide in you, ask for whatever you wish, and it will be done for you."

REFLECTIONS

In the section on FAITH, *we learned that it's really about being confident in what we're praying and hoping for. However, you may wonder, "If God already knows what we need and want, why do we still need to pray for it?" The reason is,* we *grow when we learn to be confident that God hears our prayers. We're learning daily to trust His Word, which is His rock-solid promise, that He delivers on every time!*

List 10 things below that you need or want. I challenge you to keep this list in front of you, continually praying and believing, and jot down the date when each one is manifested in your life!

_____

_____

_____

Use Me For Your Glory

LORD, use me as a vessel for Your glory. Use my creative gifts to touch someone's heart. Mold my desires so that my life is not driven by the ambition of being famous, but the pursuit of my purpose. Show me who I am in You. Give me the courage to walk out the unique calling You've placed on my life. Help me to realize that my good, bad, and ugly experiences are just ingredients in Your hands that make up an awesome finished product which will positively affect the lives of others. Make me a vessel of hope, love, healing, and restoration. It is my desire to please You with my life. In Jesus' name... Amen.

Colossians 1:10 NRSV
"... so that you may lead lives worthy of the Lord, fully pleasing to him, as you bear fruit in every good work and as you grow in the knowledge of God"

Jeremiah 18:6 NRSV
"Can I not do with you, O house of Israel, just as this potter has done? says the Lord. Just like the clay in the potter's hand, so are you in my hand, O house of Israel."

REFLECTIONS

"Less of me and more of You, Lord."

The thought of God "using us" may be a frightening thing, but in actuality, it is one of the purest intentions we can have, reminding us that we are not our own. We are alive for a purpose. God's purpose.

What would happen if you prayed this prayer at some point every day?

Take a few moments to reflect on this statement and write down what it means to you.

_____

_____

_____

Maturity (For the Young Adult)

GOD, I need to be more mature in how I live and in how I deal with other people. I may be young, but I want to conduct myself as a mature young adult. Help me to realize the benefit of adulthood and that I am meant to put away the childish ways and grow over time. I know that maturing doesn't have to mean giving up fun. Help me to not be afraid of responsibility, and help me to step up to the plate at home, in my community, in my school, and in my church. Use every experience to teach me how to live and grow up to be a better person every day. Amen.

1 Corinthians 13:11 NRSV
"When I was a child, I spoke like a child, I thought like a child, I reasoned like a child; when I became an adult, I put an end to childish ways."

REFLECTIONS

Growing up as a creative can be challenging. I know first hand the pressure of being young and gifted. Yes, life is real, but adulthood doesn't have to scare you. In our society, people tend to see creative people as immature, irresponsible, untrustworthy, and whole list of other negative qualities. Let this prayer help you counteract the stereotype.

List three (3) areas of your life that you lack maturity in. Pray about these things and start making gradual steps towards improving them. Ask a parent, family member, friend or mentor who can walk with you through your process.

_____

_____

_____

Professionalism

LORD, I pray for a mindset of professionalism. You've given me the musical and creative gifts, but I realize it's up to me to carry myself in the way that will sustain them in the world and in the marketplace. Show me the areas where I have been unprofessional and help me to listen to constructive criticism, even when it hurts. Point me to the right principles that will assist me in my journey. Send me [to] mentors that will help cultivate the professional inside of me. In Jesus' name... Amen.

Colossians 3:23-24 NLT
"Work willingly at whatever you do, as though you were working for the Lord rather than for people. Remember that the Lord will give you an inheritance as your reward, and that the Master you are serving is Christ."

REFLECTIONS

Professionalism is one of the keys to long-term success in whatever you do. Let's not just seek to be talented without the character or professionalism to support it.

"To be an outstanding musician, you have to be very attentive to the smallest detail and willing to have infinite patience in the pursuit of your ideal. You require absolute control and professionalism."
-Yehudi Menuhin

"Being a professional is doing the things you love to do, on the days you don't feel like doing them."
-Julius Irving

Write down any thoughts or feelings here.

_____

_____

_____

Integrity

LORD, teach me to have integrity. Help me to be the same person on stage and off stage, in public and in private, with no duality or hidden life. Keep me pure with a strong moral conviction that is based on Your Word. Teach me also how to make a commitment and keep my word to my family, my peers, supervisors and bosses, no matter what. Thank You for the grace to deal fairly with others and operate honestly in my business matters.
In Jesus' name... Amen.

Proverbs 11:3 NLT
"Honesty guides good people; dishonesty destroys treacherous people."

REFLECTIONS

One with Integrity can always enjoy a life of peace and experience the amazing blessings of God. Integrity isn't perfection, but it is <u>intentional</u>. In this fallen world, there will always be negative forces pulling at us (morally, spiritually, and emotionally), but we have the power to overcome it all, if we're focused and make the everyday decision to be a person of integrity.

Pause and reflect on this. Let God reveal His heart for you in this moment. Write down any helpful thoughts or what you may hear or sense.

_____

_____

_____

Creativity

GOD, thank You for making me a Creative! I am grateful for the gifts and talents that I possess. Help me to use them to their greatest potential. Continue to give me a greater capacity to think and feel, and more expansive creativity overall. Sometimes I get stuck in a rut and don't know how to get out. Open my mind, my heart, and my ears to new and fresh ideas every day. Give me a clear mind and sharpened focus. Show me things I've never seen before and grant me the creative ability to show it to the world. Amen.

Ephesians 2:10 NRSV
"For we are what he has made us, created in Christ Jesus for good works, which God prepared beforehand to be our way of life."

REFLECTIONS

We were created in the image and likeliness of The Master Creator, therefore, we have endless potential and infinite creativity within. I've learned that when I stop, listen, focus and trust, I am able to tap in to this well – not when I try to rush or make everything happen all at once. Don't pressure yourself when you feel stuck on an idea. You'll find that if you start creating (piece-by-piece) in small ways, you will end up with the full puzzle connected... A MasterPiece.

Write a few Encouraging Notes to Yourself below:

_____

_____

_____

Sounds of the Heart, Volume 1: Prayers for Musicians

My Affirmation:

I am a limitless fountain of creativity,
ideas, and inspiration.
I always have fresh vision
and motivation.
My Possibilities are Endless!

Proper Alignment (Priorities)

LORD, I need to get my priorities in order! I want to be in proper alignment and experience my best life. Show me how to prioritize God first, then myself, my family, and after that, my career. Please help me with scheduling my day and with reserving regular time for You to speak to my heart. Give me consistency as I also work to prioritize my time *(spending time on the right things)*, my health *(eating the right foods for my body, getting proper rest, working out)*, my business *(creating opportunities and wealth)*, my finances *(good money management, not being wasteful)*, and my relationships *(family, friends, associates)*.
In Jesus' name... Amen.

Matthew 6:33 NRSV
"But strive first for the kingdom of God and his righteousness, and all these things will be given to you as well."

REFLECTIONS

*Just like with money, where you spend (or "sow") your **time** and **energy** is what has your greatest attention. Those things or people are your priority. As creative, let's agree to keep our lives in proper alignment. No matter how young or old you are, you can begin today aligning yourself the way God intended!*

List some key areas that you need to prioritize regularly or for a particular season in your life.

_____

_____

_____

Relationship With God

GOD, thank You for creating me and desiring a relationship with me. It's hard to conceive that the Creator of the universe is intimately aware of me and wants to be involved in my everyday life! Help me to realize that You're always present with me (Jehovah Shammah: "The Lord is there") and that I can come to You any time, any place, for any reason. You are my peace, my hiding place. You are where I find rest, safety, and strength. Thank You for loving me and continuing to show me what love really is. Help me to cherish, respect, and guard this connection, as long as I live. In Jesus' name... Amen.

1 John 4:10 NRSV

"Whoever does not love does not know God, for God is love. God's love was revealed among us in this way: God sent his only Son into the world so that we might live through him. In this is love, not that we loved God but that he loved us and sent his Son to be the atoning sacrifice for our sins."

REFLECTIONS

Our view of 'God' can vary based on how we were raised, our current environment, and ultimately by what we've chosen to believe. Most people would hardly use the term "relationship" when referring to their interaction with God. I'd like to invite you to see God as a real person (yet in spirit form), but also One who loves us (his creation) and desires to be in communion (common union) and relationship with us. Everything begins here. God IS love.

Pause and reflect on this. In what ways can you build or strengthen your relationship with God?

_____

_____

_____

Relationship With Others

LORD, thank You for friends, family, colleagues, and other connections! You've strategically connected me to specific people - some for life and others for different stages of life - to walk with one another on our journey. Help me to regard and respect my relationships. Teach me how to glean everything I can from those who walk beside me so I can become a better person. Free me from selfishness and self-serving motives. Give me the heart to support others and to remember that it's not always about me. Help me to release myself from negative relationships and environments that will only cause me harm.
In Jesus' name... Amen.

Colossians 3:12-13 NLT
"Since God chose you to be the holy people he loves, you must clothe yourselves with tenderhearted mercy, kindness, humility, gentleness, and patience. Make allowance for each other's faults, and forgive anyone who offends you. Remember, the Lord forgave you, so you must forgive others."

REFLECTIONS

Reflect on your people relationships. How can you be a better person to those you are connected to?

Feel free to write down some ways you could improve. Ask the Lord for help in these areas.

_____

_____

_____

Focus (Mindfulness)

LORD, help me to be fully focused and fully present in each moment of life. Show me how to be aware of my feelings and honor them without judgment. Help me to not obsess about my future, nor relive my past, but to fully embrace the "now". In this world of distraction, over-stimulation, multitasking, and high-stress, I commit to slowing down and taking intentional, mindful moments through God-given tools like deep breathing. Help me to also meditate on Your Word, which gives me life.
In Jesus' name... Amen.

Philippians 4:6-7 NLT
"Don't worry about anything; instead, pray about everything. Tell God what you need, and thank him for all he has done. Then you will experience God's peace, which exceeds anything we can understand. His peace will guard your hearts and minds as you live in Christ Jesus."

Psalm 94:19 TPT
"Whenever my busy thoughts were out of control, the soothing comfort of your presence calmed me down and overwhelmed me with delight."

REFLECTIONS

Slowing down our lives and taking time to focus are essential *decisions that affect our mental and emotional wellness. We were* not *created to "rise and grind" or be "team no sleep"! These are overworking ideals that our modern society has taught us, but they lead directly to burnout, stress, depression, physical health issues and even death. Decide today to release yourself from worry and stress so that you enjoy your life more and more.*

Do A Quick Mindfulness Exercise

Reconnecting with all of your senses can **ground you in the present moment**, putting a stop to racing thoughts.
This simple mindfulness technique slows your respiration rate and reduces your pulse. It helps to let your body know that there is nothing to fear.

Take just 5 minutes in a quiet space where you can be alone. Sit upright, rest your hands on top of your thighs, and make sure you're comfortable.

Take a few deep slow breaths.

Become aware of your surroundings.

Notice 5 things you see, 4 things you hear, 3 things you feel, 2 things you smell, and 1 thing you taste.

Discipline

GOD, help me in the area of discipline. I tend to spend too much time on things that have the potential to steer me away from my purpose. I'm tired of setting goals and not reaching them because I lack discipline. Your Word empowers us to live a life of focus and intentionality, so I ask for Your power to allow me to accomplish everything you've designed for me. Help me to not waste another moment on things that may even be fun but not productive. I want to make the proper investment into myself and the gifts You gave me. In Jesus' name... Amen.

Proverbs 10:17 NIV
"Whoever heeds discipline shows the way to life, but whoever ignores correction leads others astray."

REFLECTIONS

This one is a biggie for me. Learning to be disciplined has been the hardest struggle of my life. Maybe you can identify. In many cases, I've found that creatives (like you and me) have loads of inspiration and ideas but lack what it takes to actually implement them, so we often crash and end up accomplishing nothing. How do we break out of this cycle? Generally, I've learned (and I'm still learning) that we must break down our huge "to-do" list into small chunks (start with 3 items) and make steady gradual steps toward our goals, every day.

"Inspiration has a very short shelf-life without *application*."
- Todd Henry, The Accidental Creative

Jot down 3 goals you wish to prioritize and accomplish this year.

_____

_____

_____

Sounds of the Heart, Volume 1: Prayers for Musicians

My Affirmation:

I am

Disciplined, Focused,

and Driven.

Fear

GOD, I bring my fears to You - fear of people, rejection, commitment, failure, success, and any others that I experience. Please take these fears and give me faith, love, trust, and confidence. Show me all of the areas of fear in my life and where they originate from so that I can deal with them correctly. Help me to be open to talking about my fears with someone so I don't suffer in silence. By faith in Your Word, I declare that I am no longer bound by fear in Jesus' name! Amen.

2 Timothy 1:7 NKJV
"For God has not given us a spirit of fear, but of power and of love and of a sound mind."

REFLECTIONS

What do you fear? Whether it's objects, situations, or people, it's all the result of living in a fallen (sinful) world. God's word tells us that He has not called us to a life of fear. Commit today to working on your fears one-by-one with God and with a trusted friend, spiritual leader, or counselor.

List 3 (or more) major fears below, and place a star or check by one that you'd like to overcome by this time next year. Lift these to the Lord and He will give you courage.

_____

_____

_____

Pride

GOD, deliver me from negative pride. Free me from the toxic mindset of pride that causes me to look down on others I feel that I'm better than because of my talent, social or financial status, knowledge, or experience. Help me to celebrate who I am in a healthy way, without tearing others down. Show me when pride rises up in my heart - in any form - and give me the desire to change for the better. I acknowledge that all I am and all I have comes from You. In Jesus' name... Amen.

Proverbs 16:18 NKJV
"Pride goes before destruction, and a haughty spirit before a fall."

1 Corinthians 1:31 NIV
"Therefore, as it is written: 'Let the one who boasts boast in the Lord.'"

James 4:10 NKJV
"Humble yourselves in the sight of the Lord, and He will lift you up."

REFLECTIONS

To put it plainly, pride can kill. Our dreams. Our progression. Our purity. Our relationships. Our lives. There's nothing wrong with being confident in your ability, however, pride seeks to destroy by keeping us in a negative space, constantly comparing who we are and what we have with others. As gifted creatives, let us always remember that our gifts, talents, and strengths were given to us to be used for a purpose on this earth! Our responsibility is to grow and develop what we have into something even greater, but with humility and confidence in The Creator.

Pause and Think about any areas of pride you may be dealing with, and submit them to the Lord.

_____

_____

_____

Forgiveness

GOD, I come to You asking for forgiveness for my sins - sins against You, sins against others, sins against myself. Please give me the strength to forgive people who have offended and hurt me in the past. Show me the areas in my life where I need to forgive, and give me the ability to do just that. Help me to begin overcoming my own past failures by forgiving myself and pushing forward. Jesus, thank You for giving Your life so that I can be free from my sins. By faith I receive Your forgiveness! Thank You for Your grace. I no longer walk with this weight on me. I am free!
In Jesus' name... Amen.

Matthew 5:23-24 NRSV
"So when you are offering your gift at the altar, if you remember that your brother or sister has something against you, leave your gift there before the altar and go; first be reconciled to your brother or sister, and then come and offer your gift."

REFLECTIONS

In the Bible, Jesus taught that if we are seeking forgiveness, we must also forgive (Matthew 6:14-15). It's not always possible to forget what happened, but we can, through God's strength, forgive and eventually let go. Forgiveness is more about you and your freedom than it is about the other person.

> "Forgiveness is me giving up my right to hurt you for hurting me." - Anonymous

Think about any situations in your life in which forgiveness is needed and challenge yourself to let go of the offense. Write your thoughts and emotions down as you meditate or pray, and allow God to hear and heal your heart.

_____

_____

_____

Expansion (Something Greater)

GOD, I'm ready for something new... something fresh...something bigger! I know there's something greater for me. Thank You for developing and preparing me where I am. Give me a clear direction for my next level and help me to pay attention to what You are saying to me. At the right time, I will move as You direct me. In Jesus' Name... Amen.

1 Chronicles 4:10 NRSV

"Jabez called on the God of Israel, saying, "Oh that you would bless me and enlarge my border, and that your hand might be with me, and that you would keep me from hurt and harm!" And God granted what he asked."

Philippians 1:6 NRSV

"I am confident of this, that the one who began a good work among you will bring it to completion by the day of Jesus Christ."

REFLECTIONS

We all have dreams and aspirations, things that we'd like to accomplish in our careers. I know exactly how it feels to reach a place of dissatisfaction, wondering, "What's next?" Well, I learned that when I prayed, God heard me; and it's almost as if He was waiting on ME to ask for something greater so that He could grant it. And God did! So don't be afraid to dream and then PRAY for expansion in your life!

Pray, then take the next step and write down the vision you want God to manifest! I'm sure it will take more room, so feel free to go off the page!

_____

_____

_____

Finances

LORD, I'm in need of financial help. Thank You for being my God who provides with all sufficiency. You know my needs and You know what I will pray for even before I speak. Nothing can arise in my life that You don't already know about. So, I thank You in advance for money coming in from every direction. Thank You that every bill and debt is paid in full. Thank You for unexpected checks in the mail, raises, and bonuses! Thank You for giving me the power to create wealth and for opening up special opportunities tailor-made for me to use my gifts and receive worthy compensation. I thank You that my finances will be able to fund my dreams and goals. Give me the desires that line up with Your Will, and I will always honor You with my resources.
In Jesus' name... Amen.

2 Corinthians 9:8 NRSV
"And God is able to make all grace abound toward you, that you, always having all sufficiency in all things, may have an abundance for every good work."

REFLECTIONS

"...But my God shall supply all your need according to his riches in glory by Christ Jesus." – Philippians 4:19

List your current most important financial needs or desires below, trusting God that He sees and that He will take care of your needs (and you).

_____

_____

_____

Sounds of the Heart, Volume 1: Prayers for Musicians

My Affirmation:

I am financially *free*!
My *gifts* make room for me and bring me before great people! God has *already provided* everything I need to thrive!
I have the *power to create* wealth and it is *attracted* to me!

Singleness

LORD, give me the grace to live as a single person in this society. Help me to embrace my singleness as a blessing and not a curse. Grant me your strength to live in purity and to move with integrity, knowing that I belong to You. Show me the path to my purpose while I am single, so that if or when I am married I will have already made steps toward it. I pray that You would help me to steward this season well, for Your glory, making the most of every opportunity to serve You with complete devotion. In Jesus' name... Amen.

1 Corinthians 6:19-20
"...Do you not know that your body is the temple of the Holy Spirit, within you, which you have from God? You are not your own; you were bought with a price. So glorify God in your body."

1 Corinthians 7:32-35 NIV
"I would like you to be free from concern. An unmarried man is concerned about the Lord's affairs—how he can please the Lord. But a married man is concerned about the affairs of this world—how he can please his wife— and his interests are divided. An unmarried woman or virgin is concerned about the Lord's affairs: Her aim is to be devoted to the Lord in both body and spirit. But a married woman is concerned about the affairs of this world—how she can please her husband. I am saying this for your own good, not to restrict you, but that you may live in a right way in undivided devotion to the Lord."

REFLECTIONS

Where your focus goes, there your energy flows. Rather than spending every moment concentrating on not *being married or dating, try to focus on all of the <u>benefits</u> of being single at this time in your life. It may surprise you... Know that God has an amazing plan for you!*

What are the positive things about singleness that you could focus on? List them below.

_____

_____

_____

Marriage (For Spouses)

GOD, help me to be the husband/wife You've designed me to be. Help me to love, honor, and respect my spouse. Show me how to cover him/her in prayer as he/she leads and contributes to our family naturally and spiritually. Show my spouse that they are desirable, adequate, strong, wise, and that they are my equal, bringing a wealth of greatness, expertise, and grace to my life. Cause me to see his/her abilities as a blessing, not a threat. Help me to learn and practice balance in my marriage so that my spouse doesn't feel second to my music, my children, or any other personal aspiration. Give me what I need to affirm, support, provide, and care for him/her, even when times are tough… In Jesus' name… Amen.

1 Corinthians 13:4-7 NLT

"Love is patient and kind. Love is not jealous or boastful or proud or rude. It does not demand its own way. It is not irritable, and it keeps no record of being wronged. It does not rejoice about injustice but rejoices whenever the truth wins out. Love never gives up, never loses faith, is always hopeful, and endures through every circumstance."

REFLECTIONS

Marriage is wonderfully beautiful. Marriage is also challenging work and needs the consistent covering of prayer. Keeping God at the center is essential to building a strong healthy marriage the way God intended it to be. Pray together (and for each other), worship together, serve together (and each other) and start enjoying the benefits!

What are some more specific things you are praying about regarding your spouse and your marriage? Don't forget to consider the positives!

_____

_____

_____

As A Parent

GOD, thank You for the privilege of being a parent. Thank You for blessing me with an amazing child (amazing children). Thank You for the continual strength You give me to take on this task. Give me Your grace so I won't ever take my responsibility lightly. Show me (us) how to be a good parent(s). Reveal who You have destined my child to be on this earth and help me (us) to steer him/her in that direction. If any musical or creative interest is shown, give me (us) the ability and the wisdom to harness it so their talent can be developed. Please protect and cover my child(ren) every day as they go about life, in school, at work, and as they hang with their friends. Help me to support my child, listen to my child, trust my child, nurture, and guide my child in all things and in all situations. In Jesus' name... Amen.

Proverbs 22:6 NRSV
"Train children in the right way, and when old, they will not stray."

REFLECTIONS

We need more awesome parents in this world. Be a Musician who is present, loving, responsible with, and inspiring to your children. Speak life into them every day. No matter what the circumstances are, aim to be that standard-setting role model in your child's life. Thank You, Lord for the gift of parenthood!

List 3-5 ways you will strive to be a better parent.

_____

_____

_____

As A Leader

LORD, I pray for the grace to be a great leader. Thank You for trusting me with those I lead, whether in musical endeavors, in business, in ministry or within my family. Help me to love *people* more than *policies, position,* and *power*. Help me to be more concerned with my team's success than my own. Allow me to continue gaining knowledge in the area of leadership. Never let me lose sight of the principle of servanthood. Lord, give me the heart to glean from other great leaders so I can continue to grow and help others to do the same. In Jesus' name... Amen.

Matthew 20:25-26 NLT
"But Jesus called them together and said, "You know that the rulers in this world lord it over their people, and officials flaunt their authority over those under them. But among you it will be different. Whoever wants to be a leader among you must be your servant"

REFLECTIONS

3 Powerful Quotes on Leadership
by John C. Maxwell

"A leader who produces other leaders multiplies their influences."

"Real leadership is being the person others will gladly and confidently follow."

"A leader is great, not because of his or her power, but because of his or her ability to empower others."

Write any thoughts about your leadership here.

_____

_____

_____

For A Friend

GOD, I come to You on behalf of my friend, [Insert Name Here] who really needs You right now. You know all about us and see everything we face. You are our Deliverer and our Helper in times of trouble. Please give my friend Your peace, joy, comfort, and strength. Let them feel Your love right now, in Jesus' name. Amen.

Psalm 46:1 KJV
"God is our refuge and strength, a very present help in trouble."

Proverbs 17:17 NIV
"A friend loves at all times, and a brother is born for adversity."

REFLECTIONS

Take time and meditate on what you just prayed. Believe that God has heard you, and receive the answered prayer in your heart.

If you wish, list any other friends who are in need of prayer. God sees and knows.

_____

_____

_____

For My Family

GOD, I pray right now for my family. Keep us close and continue to knit our hearts together. Help us to care for each other and love each other. Bless them in every area of need. Please watch over them and protect them. Let Your love shine from within us and help us to honor You as a family. Amen.

Acts 10:2 MSG
"He was a thoroughly good man. He had led everyone in his house to live worshipfully before God, was always helping people in need, and had the habit of prayer."

Psalm 5:11 NRSV
"But let all who take refuge in you rejoice, let them ever sing for joy. Spread your protection over them, so that those who love your name may exult in you."

REFLECTIONS

Being part of a family is a true blessing. So many people take this for granted and don't realize how privileged they are to experience life with those that love and care for them. If you're fortunate to have had any type of family, show your gratitude by praying for them often. If you don't have family around, know that you're loved and that someone is praying for you! May God bless you and surround you with a community of amazing people!

What family members are you grateful for and will commit to praying for?

_____

_____

_____

True Success

LORD, help me to learn and seek after what true success really is - accomplishing my God-given purpose. As a musician (creative artist), it's so easy to get lured into the wrong mindset about success. I don't want to chase dreams and goals just for fame and money. Help me to chase after my purpose faithfully, and be true to who I am. With Your help, I can be confident that success (the way You design it for me) will come in time. Free me from the pressures of other people's opinions and thoughts. Teach me how to see myself as successful, no matter what.
In Jesus' name... Amen.

Proverbs 16:3 NIV
"Commit to the Lord whatever you do, and he will establish your plans."

REFLECTIONS

The subject of God-given purpose is such a huge one to me. It's so important, especially as musicians and creative artists that we understand who we were made to be (individually). True success flows from this place... Let us not allow the world around us to define success – money, cars, homes, big contracts, touring with major artists, our music being featured in movies. All of that is great, but please know that the people who reach those pinnacle success points are those who have embraced their uniqueness and built upon it. Find out and be comfortable with who you are and then offer what you have to help change the world through your art!

Pause and Reflect on this. Feel free to write down any notes.

_____

_____

_____

Influence

GOD, I recognize that You've created us all to have influence in some unique way. Show me how to use the influence I have in the right way. Help me to be mindful of everything I do, say, post, like, view.... and remind me that I'm being studied by many people I may never meet or talk to. Allow my life – both the ups and downs – to weave together a story that impacts everyone You've placed within my circle of influence. Let that story point people back to You. In Jesus' name... Amen.

Matthew 5:13-14 NIV
"You are the salt of the earth; but if the salt has become tasteless, how can it be made salty again? It is no longer good for anything, except to be thrown out and trampled under foot by men. "You are the light of the world..."

REFLECTIONS

What we do today will directly affect our tomorrow and the next generation coming behind us, so we must always remember who we are. How will you use your influence from now on?

Write down (3) of your most influential qualities.

_____

_____

_____

Sounds of the Heart, Volume 1: Prayers for Musicians

My Affirmation:

I am a *resource* for others and a conduit of blessings. I am *blessed* to be a blessing and walk in God's true purpose for my *influence*.

Healing (For Sickness & Disease)

GOD, I come to You believing that You are the Healer, Jehovah Rapha ("God who heals"). It is Your power that makes us whole, so I bring this sickness to You, the Omniscient (all-knowing) God. Thank You for Your sacrifice of blood that guarantees our healing. Your Word has given us the authority to speak what we believe in faith, so I speak total healing and recovery to my [or insert friend or family member's name here] physical body and mind. Let Your healing virtue flow to me [or friend's or family member's name] right now, in Jesus' name. Thank you for total recovery!
Amen.

Jeremiah 17:14
"Heal me, O Lord, and I will be healed; save me and I will be saved, for you are the one I praise."

Psalm 103:2-4
"Praise the LORD, my soul, and forget not all his benefits - who forgives all your sins and heals all your diseases, who redeems your life from the pit and crowns you with love and compassion."

REFLECTIONS

The Supernatural, healing power of God is available to us when we place our faith in Jesus. Trust and believe and healing is ours!

Write down any physical conditions or illnesses you are seeking healing for. You can also write the names of family members, friends, or others who need healing.

_____

_____

_____

Depression

GOD, I am reaching out to You. I feel alone and I'm not sure about anything right now. Life just isn't making sense. I've lost my energy and sometimes I don't want to get out of bed to face the world. I need You! Please let Your peace cover my mind and let Your love to fill my heart. Protect me. Send the right people to help me. Give me the strength to open up to a family member, a close friend, church leader, or a professional counselor. Lord, please remove the clouds in my mind and emotions and cause me to see things from Your divine perspective, in Jesus' name... Amen.

Philippians 4:8 MSG
"Summing it all up, friends, I'd say you'll do best by filling your minds and meditating on things true, noble, reputable, authentic, compelling, gracious—the best, not the worst; the beautiful, not the ugly; things to praise, not things to curse. Put into practice what you learned from me, what you heard and saw and realized. Do that, and God, who makes everything work together, will work you into his most excellent harmonies."

REFLECTIONS

Depression is a huge enemy of the creative artist. It has the potential to immobilize us and stunt our creative growth. We can experience depression as a result of negative events or trauma, or we could be clinically depressed and need medical and psychological help. Musicians, if you're struggling with this enemy, there's hope. I've experienced depression as a teen and multiple times as an adult. It's not pretty; therefore, we must do our best to counteract it with prayer, counseling, affirmation, meditation, and just having fun!

Refer back to the <u>Gratitude Prayer</u> whenever you begin feeling depressed. Grab your instrument and start singing songs of praise or joyful songs & melodies. Go out for a walk and focus on the beauty of nature. Do something fun. Allow yourself to laugh, even in the hard times.

Suicidal Thoughts

STOP RIGHT HERE! If you're thinking about harming yourself, CALL THE **NATIONAL SUICIDE PREVENTION LIFELINE: 1-800-273-8255** and speak to someone that can help you through this difficult time. YOU CAN DO THIS!

God, the darkness has taken hold me and I can't find my way back to the light. At this moment, ending it all seems like the best option, the only option, and the only way to escape. Yet, I feel like there is something in me that wants Your light to destroy this darkness. So I ask that you would do just that. Remind me that when I feel hopeless, You have hope **in me** and **for me**. Remind me that I am **seen, heard** and **deeply loved**. Give me the desire to live! When I feel like I don't matter, remind me that I was created with a **purpose**. When I don't know or understand why I feel the way I feel, remind me that You know the depth of the pain in my heart, in my body and in my being. Help me to know You still have **great plans for my life**. Remind me that I am **fearfully and wonderfully made**, and <u>I am worth more</u> than I know.
In Jesus' name... Amen.

Isaiah 41:10 NIV

"So do not fear, for I am with you; do not be dismayed, for I am your God. I will strengthen you and help you; I will uphold you with my righteous right hand."

Psalm 34:18, 19 NIV

"The LORD is close to the brokenhearted and saves those who are crushed in spirit. A righteous man may have many troubles, but the Lord delivers him from them all."

REFLECT:

Sit or lay and take a few minutes to breathe several deep breaths. Take in God's loving presence.

Please Call the National Suicide Prevention Lifeline: 1-800-273-8255

{*Prayer adapted from 'A Prayer for Fighting Suicidal Thoughts' by Beth Ann Baus; Crosswalk.com*}

Overcoming Addictions

GOD, I come to you needing freedom. I am addicted to [speak out your addiction struggle(s) here]. I can't hide anymore. I don't know how to help myself. I've tried to stop myself day after day, month after month, year after year... and every time, I end up right back where I started. I call out to YOU now because I believe that YOU alone have the power to heal and set me free. Please forgive me of these sins. Forgive me for trying to take matters into my own hands and using my addictions to mask and medicate the underlying issues in my heart: hurt, disappointment, inadequacy, loneliness, and shame. Lord, please make me whole again and start me on the pathway to freedom. In Jesus' name... Amen.

1 Corinthians 10:13 ESV
"No temptation has overtaken you that is not common to man. God is faithful, and he will not let you be tempted beyond your ability, but with the temptation he will also provide the way of escape, that you may be able to endure it."

REFLECTIONS

Addiction can take various forms, all detrimental to our lives. Whatever your addiction and whatever the source of it - Drugs, Alcohol, Pornography, Sex, Food, Social Media - you can experience freedom today. I can tell you personally as a 20-year addiction survivor that this is true. My life has never been the same! I pray that the Lord would reveal any areas of addiction and negative habits to you so that you can be a better you. Seek God now. He's open, He's waiting, and He is listening. Seek counseling. There are amazing therapists available to help you walk into a path of freedom.

Helpful Link -
https://www.psychologytoday.com

Pause and think. Reflect and write.

_____

_____

_____

Confidence in My Identity
(for Low Self-Image)

LORD, help me to see myself the way You see me. For so many reasons, I have not tapped into the strength to stand confidently in my true identity. These reasons may seem valid to me, but because You're the One who created me, they may be an insult to You. Please forgive me! Help me to stop comparing myself to other people – my physical qualities, my creative abilities, my accomplishments, what I have and have not experienced – help me stop the comparison game! Show me that I'm carving out my own path and that it's okay to be different. Give me the desire and discipline to spend more time in Your Word than on social media or in other environments that cause me to doubt who I am, based on what others portray. Help me to realize that I am enough and that I have enough because I'm Your child.
In Jesus' name... Amen.

Psalm 139:14 NIV
*"I praise you because I am fearfully and
wonderfully made; your works are wonderful, I know that full well."*

REFLECTIONS

Low self-image, lack of confidence, and lack of identity seem to be common among Creatives. We receive the applause of people in response to our talents, but we often struggle behind the scenes with not feeling truly known or accepted for who we are outside of our abilities. Let God shower you with His LOVE today, washing your minds and hearts of the feelings of inadequacy and self-doubt. You are seen. You are known. You are loved. You are significant. You are enough.

Write your own affirmation statements below.
("I am...")

_____

_____

_____

Sounds of the Heart, Volume 1: Prayers for Musicians

My Affirmation:

I am God's prized possession, created in His image.

Wonderfully made.

I AM ENOUGH.

Sounds of the Heart, Volume 1: Prayers for Musicians

A MUSICIAN'S PRAYER

Divine Composer, I start this day on a joyful note, thanking You for all the blessings You have orchestrated in my life. Help me to live in harmony with others throughout the day. May I be Your instrument, in concert with Your will and in tune with Your way – trusting I always have You as my accompaniment. And at day's end, may I know that I have played my part to put a song in every heart. Amen.

-Unknown

Acknowledgments

I thank God, the Master Author, without whom none of what I do would be possible. This book was birthed from Your heart to mine. I'm overwhelmed at how You love me.

Again, the hugest thanks to my wife Brittany and our immediate and extended families.

To Dr. Hart Ramsey, for yet again contributing something amazing to what God has inspired me to do. For your wisdom, profound knowledge, and for being a genuine person... I appreciate you!

To Robin Ware, my success coach, who knew I'd ever be an author?! Thanks for pushing me when I didn't want to be pushed. This is just the beginning!

To Chantea Williams at Relentless Publishing House, LLC. for your push, your patience, and your positivity throughout this process, I really appreciate you.

To graphic designer Justin Foster, thanks as always for the awesome creative work and helping to envision Sounds of the Heart!

THANK YOU to every Mentor, Pastor, Choir Director, Minister of Music, Musician, Vocalist, Recording Artist, Producer, and member of every local church and international organization that I've had the pleasure to serve with. I'm grateful for your hand in my development over the course of my life.

ABOUT THE AUTHOR

Trent Phillips is regarded as one of the music industry's most notable professional Keyboardists, Musical Directors and Producers. For over 20 years, he has performed on award-winning albums, major stages across the world, and on TV and film platforms with many famed Gospel & Christian industry artists. Trent serves as a mentor for musicians, locally and abroad, also using his experience to aid churches, organizations, and individuals as a Consultant in areas of Worship, Leadership Development, Musicianship, Music Production and Artistry. Trent Phillips is the CEO of Lionheart Music Productions, Inc., and resides in Atlanta, Georgia with his lovely wife, Brittany, a licensed professional counselor and trauma educator.

www.trentphillips.com

Sounds of the Heart, Volume 1: Prayers for Musicians

Sounds of the Heart, Volume 1: Prayers for Musicians

Sounds of the Heart, Volume 1: Prayers for Musicians

www.ingramcontent.com/pod-product-compliance
Lightning Source LLC
Chambersburg PA
CBHW031202090426
42736CB00009B/759